# my big dinosaur world

## Simon Mugford

### Illustrations by John Francis

priddy books

big ideas for little people

# Contents

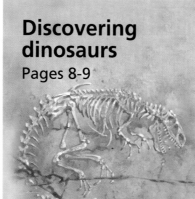
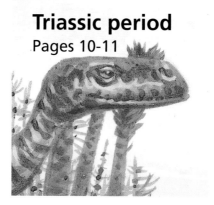
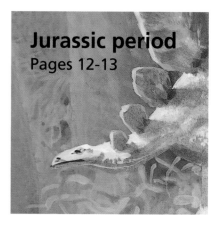

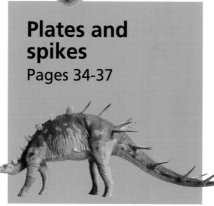

Edited by Hermione Edwards and Natalie Boyd
Designed by Holly Russell
Models created by Graham High and Gary Kings

Copyright © 2008 St. Martin's Press, LLC
175 Fifth Avenue, New York, NY 10010

Created for St. Martin's Press by
priddy books

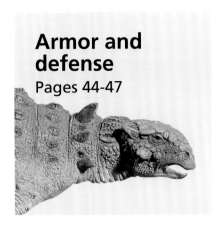
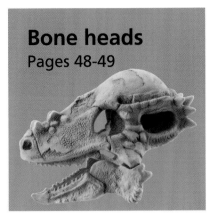

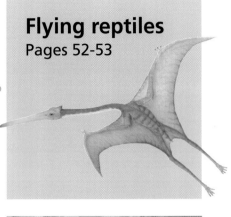

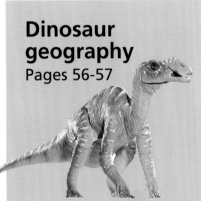
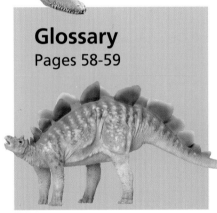

# Discovering dinosaurs

Dinosaurs were a group of incredibly varied reptiles that dominated life on Earth for over 150 million years. These ancient creatures have fascinated people since evidence of them was first discovered almost 200 years ago. In this book, artists' illustrations and models help us to imagine the life, look and behavior of these amazing reptiles.

## Digging dinosaurs

We can find out about dinosaurs by studying their fossils. Fossils are the remains of living things, which have turned into rock over millions of years. They are dug up and studied by scientists called paleontologists.

A paleontologist uncovers a fossil at a dinosaur dig

## Fossil finds

The best places to look for fossils are areas where rock from millions of years ago has been exposed – such as cliffs, seashores and rocky deserts. By studying dinosaur fossils, and comparing their findings with creatures that are alive today, paleontologists are able to develop ideas about how dinosaurs looked and moved, what they ate and how they lived and died.

Fossils of complete dinosaur skeletons are extremely rare. Usually only a small number of fossilized bones or skulls are discovered

## Dinosaurs up close

One of the best ways to learn about dinosaurs is to visit one of the many museums around the world with displays dedicated to these incredible creatures. The best exhibitions have life-sized reconstructions of skeletons, or models, which attempt to give visitors a very realistic impression of how the dinosaurs looked.

Face to face with a giant killer!

# Triassic period

The first dinosaurs appeared on Earth about 206 million years ago, at the end of a time named the Triassic period. This period had begun about 42 million years before with a catastrophic event that wiped out almost all of the living things on Earth. This extinction allowed new groups of animals to develop. During the early Triassic, the first amphibians and reptiles appeared. Pterosaurs (flying reptiles), icthyosaurs (marine reptiles) and the earliest mammals came later, at about the same time as the dinosaurs. The climate was generally dry and hot, but wetter conditions at the poles saw palm and fern-like plants and trees begin to grow.

Cycads

Riojasaurus

Horsetail ferns

Eodicynodon

**Riojasaurus**
This dinosaur was a very early relative of the huge, long-necked sauropods

**Horsetail ferns**
These hardy, fast-growing plants were an important source of food at this time

**Eodicynodon**
This was a dicynodont – a group of animals known as 'mammal-like reptiles'

**Cycads**
Similar to palm trees, cycads were very common throughout the Triassic period

Eudimorphodon

Coelophysis

Pisanosaurus

Crocodilian

**Eudimorphodon**
One of the first pterosaurs, it had a wingspan of around 3 feet

**Coelophysis**
This lightweight, fast runner was one of the first meat-eating dinosaurs

**Pisanosaurus**
This small, plant-eating dinosaur probably moved quickly on two legs

**Crocodilian**
The ancestors of modern crocodiles appeared during the late Triassic period

# Jurassic period

The Jurassic period, which lasted from 203 to 144 million years ago, was the time when dinosaurs became the most important animals on Earth. New types of dinosaurs, including the giant Diplodocus and big meat eaters such as Allosaurus, all appeared during the Jurassic period, as well as other famous dinosaurs such as Stegosaurus. It was during this time that the land began to drift apart and form into different continents. These land changes created new seas, coral reefs and different types of forests, where most of the life on Earth would have lived. The climate was still warm, with much less seasonal change than there is now.

Pterosaurs

Iguanodon

Stegosaurus

Diplodocus

Ornitholestes

**Pterosaurs**
Pterosaurs were common in the late Jurassic period

**Diplodocus**
The best-known of the long-necked sauropods

**Iguanodon**
This common plant eater was first found in England

**Stegosaurus**
One of several spiked, plated dinosaurs from this time

**Ornitholestes**
A small, fast meat eater – name means 'bird thief'

Archaeopteryx

Allosaurus

Coelurus

Compsognathus

**Allosaurus**
Terrifying, large
meat eaters such as
Allosaurus appeared
at this time

**Archaeopteryx**
An unusual creature
that could be a link
between dinosaurs
and birds

**Coelurus**
Another small
meat eater,
closely related to
Ornitholestes

**Compsognathus**
This tiny meat
eater was the
smallest dinosaur –
the size of a chicken

# Cretaceous period

The Cretaceous was the last period during which the dinosaurs lived on Earth. It began about 144 million years ago and ended 79 million years later with the mass extinction of the dinosaurs and many other living things. In the time leading up to that, however, the dinosaurs had become the most dominant creatures on Earth. There was a huge variety of species – from the massive, terrifying Tyrannosaurus rex and smaller predators such as Velociraptor to numerous types of herbivores such as Triceratops and families of hadrosaurs. There were many more mammals too, and the first birds also appeared at this time. Towards the end of the period the climate was changing dramatically, sea levels were dropping and there was a lot of volcanic activity.

Saltasaurus

Maiasaura

Triceratops

Oviraptor

**Saltasaurus**
A sauropod with small, bony plates on its back

**Triceratops**
The largest and most famous of the horned ceratopsians

**Oviraptor**
Small, speedy Oviraptor stole eggs from nests to eat

**Maiasaura**
A dinosaur that is known to have cared for its young

**Parasauroloph**
The most famous of the 'duckbilled' hadrosaurs

Parasaurolophus

T rex

Hadrosaurus

Deinonychus

Corythosaurus

Velociraptor

**Hadrosaurus**
The first dinosaur to be discovered in the USA

**Corythosaurus**
Another hadrosaur – its name means 'helmet lizard'

**T rex**
Bloodthirsty T rex is the most famous dinosaur

**Velociraptor**
A very quick, small predator with a sharp toe claw

**Deinonychus**
This was a slightly larger relative of Velociraptor

# Giant killers

The huge, meat-eating predators that lived around 65 million years ago were the most terrifying of all the dinosaurs. Tyrannosaurus rex – the 'king of the tyrant lizards' – lived in what is now North America, and was perhaps the most fearsome of them all.

 T rex was one of the largest of a group of dinosaurs called theropods. Tall enough to peer in through a third-story window, its huge head and massive, muscular body were balanced by its heavy, powerful tail. Many fossils of T rex have been found, suggesting that there were lots of them terrifying other dinosaurs during the late Cretaceous period.

 **Where?**
Remains of T rex have been found in North America

 **Diet**
These huge beasts ate other dinosaurs, some even bigger than themselves!

 **Habitat**
T rex probably lived in forests, where its prey would have looked for food

 **Famous fact**
The largest T rex skeleton is kept at the Field Museum in Chicago, USA

## Tyrant king

The sheer size and bulk of T rex's head added to its terrifying appearance. Its massive, extremely powerful jaws filled with hundreds of knife-sharp teeth were its most lethal weapon – its tiny arms and hands would have been of little use. T rex would probably have torn off huge chunks of flesh and bone and swallowed them whole. In fact, some experts say that Tyrannosaurus rex would certainly have been able to gobble up a human being in one gulp!

## Tyrannosaurus rex

Bony ridges along the top of its head

Very strong, muscular jaws

Large nostrils at the front of its face

Some teeth were up to 12 inches long

Mouth filled with knife-sharp teeth

Brain cavity

Eye cavity

Tyrannosaurus rex's skull

## Giant killers compared

Tyrannosaurus rex
40 feet long,
18 feet high

Allosaurus
40 feet long,
10 feet high

Carnotaurus
25 feet long,
10 feet high

**Note**
The silhouette shows a man of average height, and the dinosaurs' heights are measured to their hips, unless otherwise stated

## Hunter or scavenger?

While many dinosaur experts agree that T rex was a fast-moving hunter that preyed on healthy adult dinosaurs, others suggest that its size and weight meant that it could not move very quickly.

This could mean that it only attacked dinosaurs that were young, old or injured, or that it simply scavenged meat from creatures that were already dead.

Tyrannosaurus rex

Height (at hips): 18 feet
Length: 40 feet
Weight: 12,000 pounds

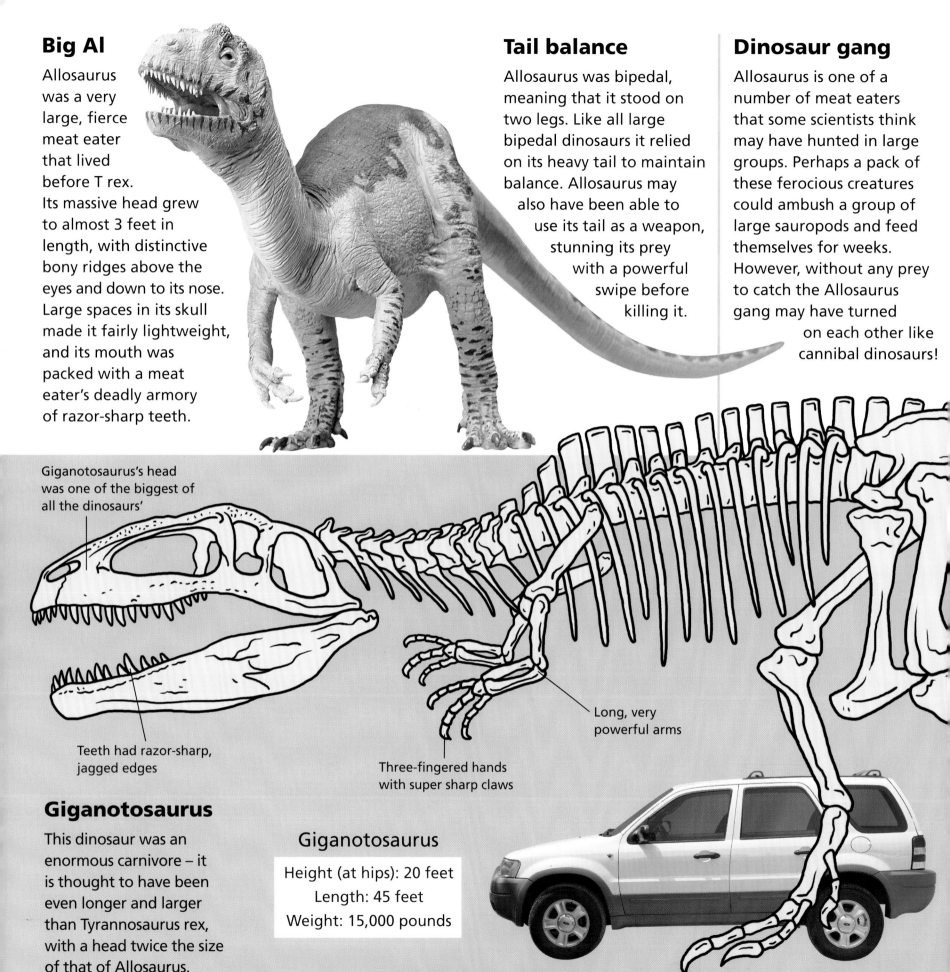

## Big Al

Allosaurus was a very large, fierce meat eater that lived before T rex. Its massive head grew to almost 3 feet in length, with distinctive bony ridges above the eyes and down to its nose. Large spaces in its skull made it fairly lightweight, and its mouth was packed with a meat eater's deadly armory of razor-sharp teeth.

## Tail balance

Allosaurus was bipedal, meaning that it stood on two legs. Like all large bipedal dinosaurs it relied on its heavy tail to maintain balance. Allosaurus may also have been able to use its tail as a weapon, stunning its prey with a powerful swipe before killing it.

## Dinosaur gang

Allosaurus is one of a number of meat eaters that some scientists think may have hunted in large groups. Perhaps a pack of these ferocious creatures could ambush a group of large sauropods and feed themselves for weeks. However, without any prey to catch the Allosaurus gang may have turned on each other like cannibal dinosaurs!

Giganotosaurus's head was one of the biggest of all the dinosaurs'

Teeth had razor-sharp, jagged edges

Long, very powerful arms

Three-fingered hands with super sharp claws

## Giganotosaurus

This dinosaur was an enormous carnivore – it is thought to have been even longer and larger than Tyrannosaurus rex, with a head twice the size of that of Allosaurus.

Giganotosaurus

Height (at hips): 20 feet
Length: 45 feet
Weight: 15,000 pounds

## Angry Allosaurus

Allosaurus is considered to be one of the most vicious and effective of the large meat eaters. With longer arms than Tyrannosaurus rex, it was probably able to grab hold of its prey as well as slash and bite with its mouth and teeth. As a lone hunter, Allosaurus would probably have been able to hunt and eat plant-eating dinosaurs about the same size as itself.

Allosaurus was an agile and effective predator, easily catching relatively large plant eaters such as Camptosaurus

Tail may have been powerful enough to stun enemies

Strong tailbones helped it keep itself balanced

## Open wide

Dinosaurs like Allosaurus were able to open their jaws as normal, but could also move them slightly apart. This meant that they could bite the biggest possible chunks out of their prey. They may even have used their jaws and teeth as weapons, slashing out at their enemies in fights, and for attacking their unfortunate prey.

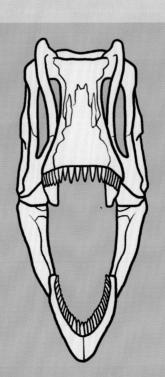
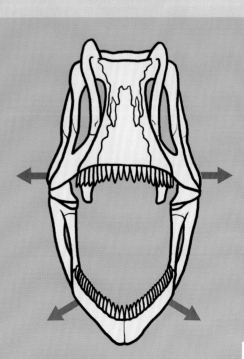

19

## Dinosaur bulls

The remains of some of the more unusual types of large meat eaters have been discovered in South America. Carnotaurus, which means 'meat-eating bull', had a much shorter and deeper head than Allosaurus or Tyrannosaurus rex. It also had bull-like horns above its eyes, and rows of tough, rounded scales that ran in rows along its back.

Scaly bumps may have protected it

A short, thick bony horn above each eye

## Carnotaurus

Nostrils at the front of its head

Long, sharp, slender teeth

Carnotaurus, the bull dinosaur

## Bony relations

Ceratosaurus was a close relative of Allosaurus, but like Carnotaurus, it had rows of unusual plates along its body and tail. Some scientists have suggested that such plates helped make it appear superior to its rivals, or perhaps even more terrifying to its prey. The Stegosaurus pictured right, and other dinosaurs of its type, would certainly have found the large meat eaters like Ceratosaurus and Carnotaurus very frightening, whether they had horns or not!

## Eyes forward

Carnotaurus's eyes faced a little more forward than those of many other meat eaters. This may have meant it had good eyesight, helping it hunt more effectively.

### Carnotaurus

Height (at hips): 10 feet
Length: 25 feet
Weight: 2,000 pounds

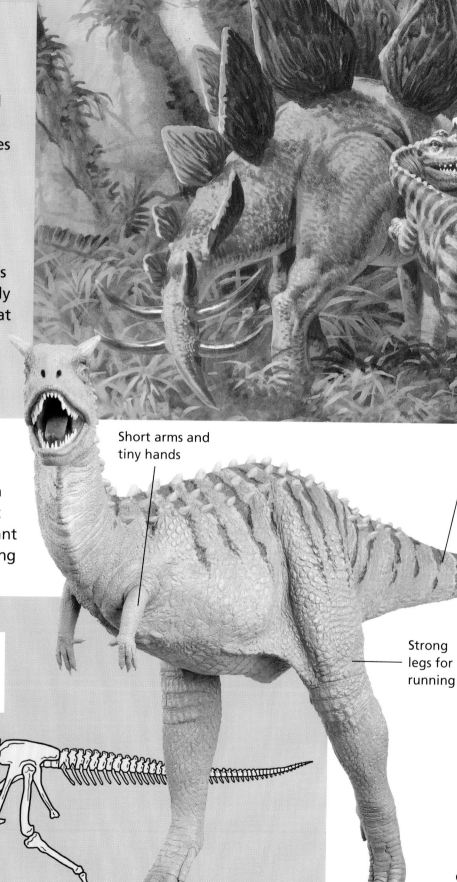

Short arms and tiny hands

Powerful tail probably helped it balance

Strong legs for running

Clawed toes to hold and tear its food

## Little hands

Carnotaurus had very short arms and tiny hands, smaller even than those of Tyrannosaurus rex. This means that Carnotaurus and others like it would probably have attacked their prey head first, or scavenged meat from those that were already dead.

# Gentle giants

The sauropods were the largest dinosaurs of all, and the largest animals to have ever walked the Earth. These enormous plant-eating creatures appeared in the late Triassic period, but were most common in the Jurassic.

Sauropods can be roughly divided into two groups. Some, like Diplodocus and Apatosaurus, were incredibly long. They held their heads down low and had very long necks and tails. Others, such as Brachiosaurus, stood in a more upright position, and held their heads up high. They had shorter tails and would rear up on to their back legs to feed.

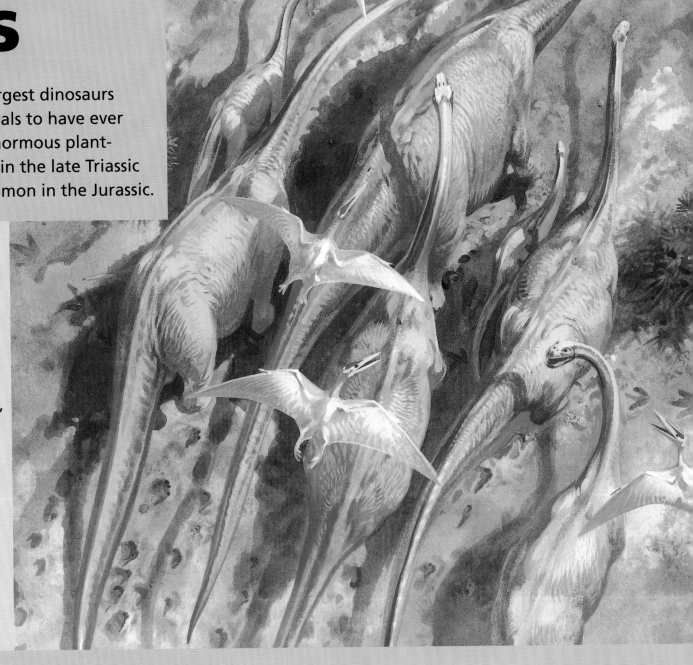

 **Where?**
The most well-known sauropod, Diplodocus, roamed throughout North America

 **Diet**
These giant creatures grazed on plants, sometimes from the tops of trees

 **Habitat**
Wooded areas that offered protection and large amounts of food

 **Famous fact**
The first skeleton of Diplodocus was discovered in Wyoming, USA

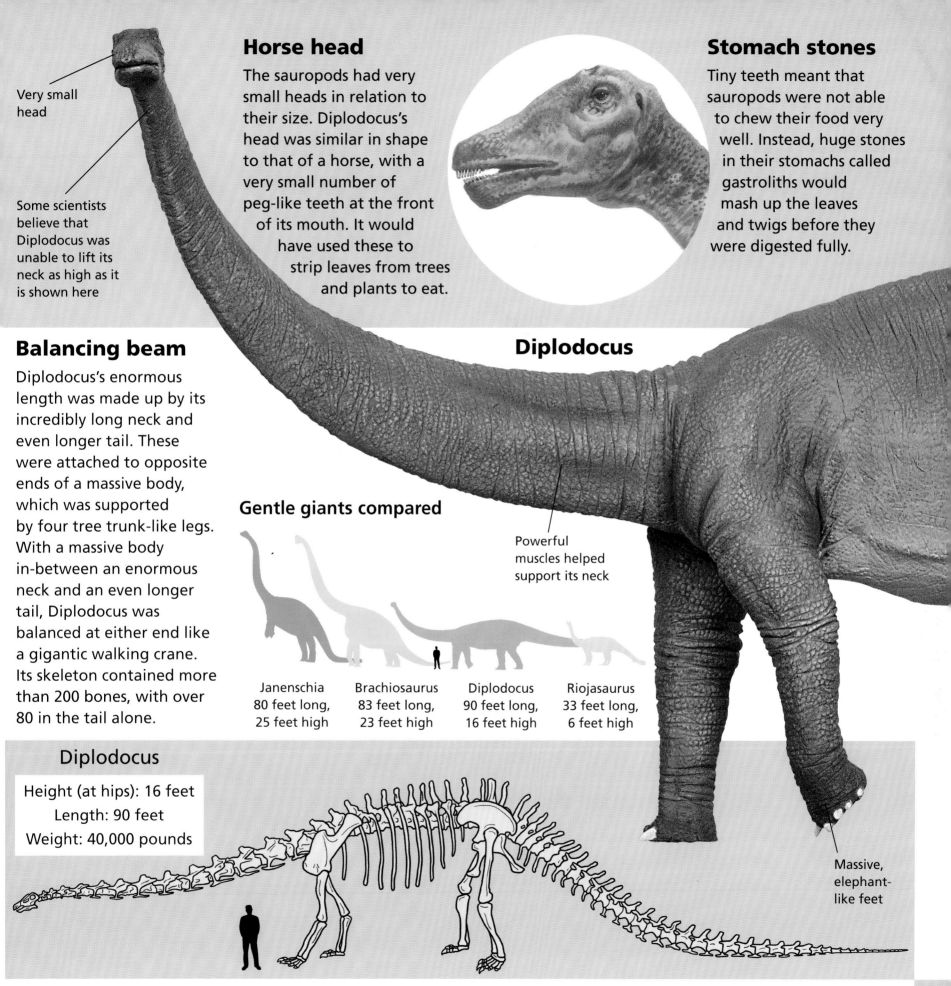

## Horse head

The sauropods had very small heads in relation to their size. Diplodocus's head was similar in shape to that of a horse, with a very small number of peg-like teeth at the front of its mouth. It would have used these to strip leaves from trees and plants to eat.

## Stomach stones

Tiny teeth meant that sauropods were not able to chew their food very well. Instead, huge stones in their stomachs called gastroliths would mash up the leaves and twigs before they were digested fully.

**Very small head**

**Some scientists believe that Diplodocus was unable to lift its neck as high as it is shown here**

## Balancing beam

Diplodocus's enormous length was made up by its incredibly long neck and even longer tail. These were attached to opposite ends of a massive body, which was supported by four tree trunk-like legs. With a massive body in-between an enormous neck and an even longer tail, Diplodocus was balanced at either end like a gigantic walking crane. Its skeleton contained more than 200 bones, with over 80 in the tail alone.

## Diplodocus

### Gentle giants compared

Janenschia
80 feet long,
25 feet high

Brachiosaurus
83 feet long,
23 feet high

Diplodocus
90 feet long,
16 feet high

Riojasaurus
33 feet long,
6 feet high

**Powerful muscles helped support its neck**

## Diplodocus

Height (at hips): 16 feet
Length: 90 feet
Weight: 40,000 pounds

**Massive, elephant-like feet**

## Skin shapes

Fossilized impressions of skin have shown that Diplodocus may have had varying bony patterns on its skin. Some may have had bony bumps, while others could have had a row of scaly spines along their backs.

## Biggest beast

The largest of all the sauropods, and one of the biggest animals ever to walk the Earth was Brachiosaurus. Standing at up to 42 feet, it lived in the late Jurassic period and is one of the most famous and widely recognized dinosaurs of all.

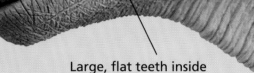

Nostrils on the top of its head

Large, flat teeth inside its mouth for chewing leaves

Diplodocus's enormous weight was mostly supported by its back legs. It may have been able to stand up on them to reach leaves up high

One toe on each foot had a large claw

## Tree grazers

Apatosaurus (pictured right) was a close relative of Diplodocus. It would probably have grazed on the twigs, leaves and branches of fir, pine and sequoia trees during the late Jurassic period.

## Walking in water?

The enormous size and bulk of the sauropods led scientists to think that they spent much of their time floating in water, in an attempt to support their massive weight. Brachiosaurus had its nostrils on the top of its head, which seemed to make this theory even more possible. However, most paleontologists now believe that this was not necessarily the case. In fact, some believe that sauropods could move surprisingly quickly, perhaps as fast as 19 mph!

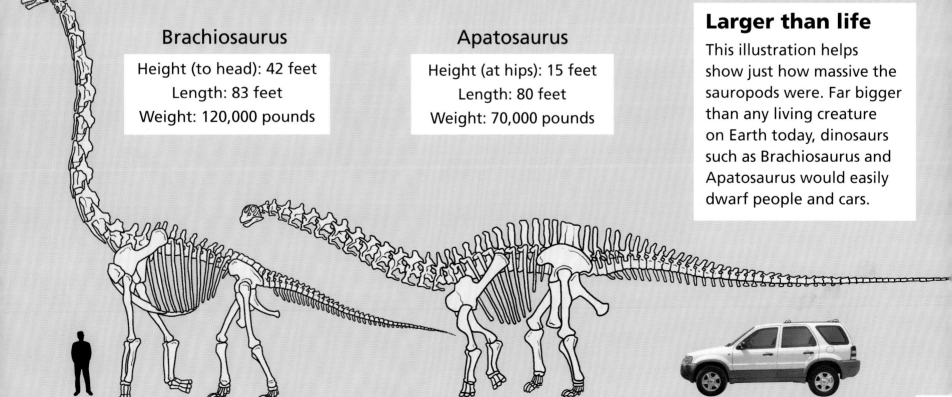

### Brachiosaurus

Height (to head): 42 feet
Length: 83 feet
Weight: 120,000 pounds

### Apatosaurus

Height (at hips): 15 feet
Length: 80 feet
Weight: 70,000 pounds

### Larger than life

This illustration helps show just how massive the sauropods were. Far bigger than any living creature on Earth today, dinosaurs such as Brachiosaurus and Apatosaurus would easily dwarf people and cars.

# Beaks and teeth

The hadrosaurs, or 'duckbills', and their earlier relative Iguanodon were the most commonly found dinosaurs. Among the first dinosaurs to be discovered, they had very distinctive mouths and teeth. They are also thought to have lived together in groups.

Fossilized nests, eggs and the remains of young Maiasaura dinosaurs were found with an adult skeleton in Montana, USA, in 1978. This was the first evidence to show that some dinosaurs may have cared for their young. It is likely that these large, plant-eating animals lived and nested together in groups, and returned to the same nesting place each year.

**Where?**
Iguanodon remains have been found in Europe; 'duckbills' lived in North America

**Diet**
These dinosaurs were vegetarian, eating leaves and plants such as ferns

**Habitat**
Forests and swamps where there was plenty of food and shelter

**Famous fact**
In 1858 Hadrosaurus was the first dinosaur to be discovered in North America

## Lizard tooth

Iguanodon, named because its teeth were similar to those of an iguana, was one of the most common dinosaurs of the late Jurassic and early Cretaceous periods. It was a large plant eater (up to 28 feet long) that could walk on four legs or two. Iguanodon had a wide, toothless beak that it used to bite into plants. It then ground up its food with the blunt teeth at the back of its mouth.

## Thumbs up

Iguanodon had five-fingered hands, with an unusual bony spike on its thumb that it may have used to collect food or to defend itself.

Iguanodons may have gathered together in groups to eat

## Iguanodons

## Safety in numbers

Dinosaurs may have lived in large groups for safety – the chance of being eaten by a predator is less if there are lots of you! Some scientists think that finding fossilized groups of dinosaurs means that they had a family 'instinct'. Others say that they simply gathered together in places where there was food.

Sharp thumb spike, which was originally thought to be a horn

## Beaks and teeth compared

| Iguanodon | Hadrosaurus | Parasaurolophus |
|-----------|-------------|-----------------|
| 28 feet long, | 30 feet long, | 40 feet long, |
| 9 feet high | 10 feet high | 8 feet high |

**Corythosaurus's** rounded head crest explains why it was named 'helmet lizard'.

**Lambeosaurus** had a crest that was shaped a bit like an ax.

**Parasaurolophus** shows the tightly-packed teeth at the back of its mouth.

## Duckbills

Hadrosaurs were later relatives of Iguanodon. They are known as 'duckbills' because of their wide, flat mouths shaped like a duck's beak. As with Iguanodon, their beaks were toothless, but they had many teeth at the back of the mouth – sometimes as many as 2,000. These would crush and grind up the plants that they ate.

## Hadrosaurus

Duck-billed Hadrosaurus was the first dinosaur to be discovered and identified in the USA.

The tail was narrow and stiff towards the end

Parasaurolophus's tail was especially broad at the base. It may have used it to signal to other dinosaurs

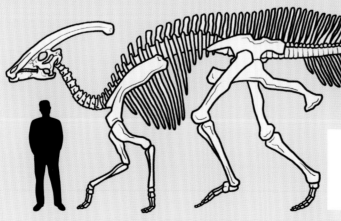

Parasaurolophus

Height (at hips): 8 feet
Length: 40 feet
Weight: 4,000 pounds

Hadrosaurs had thick, three-toed, padded feet. It seems that they walked on both two and four legs

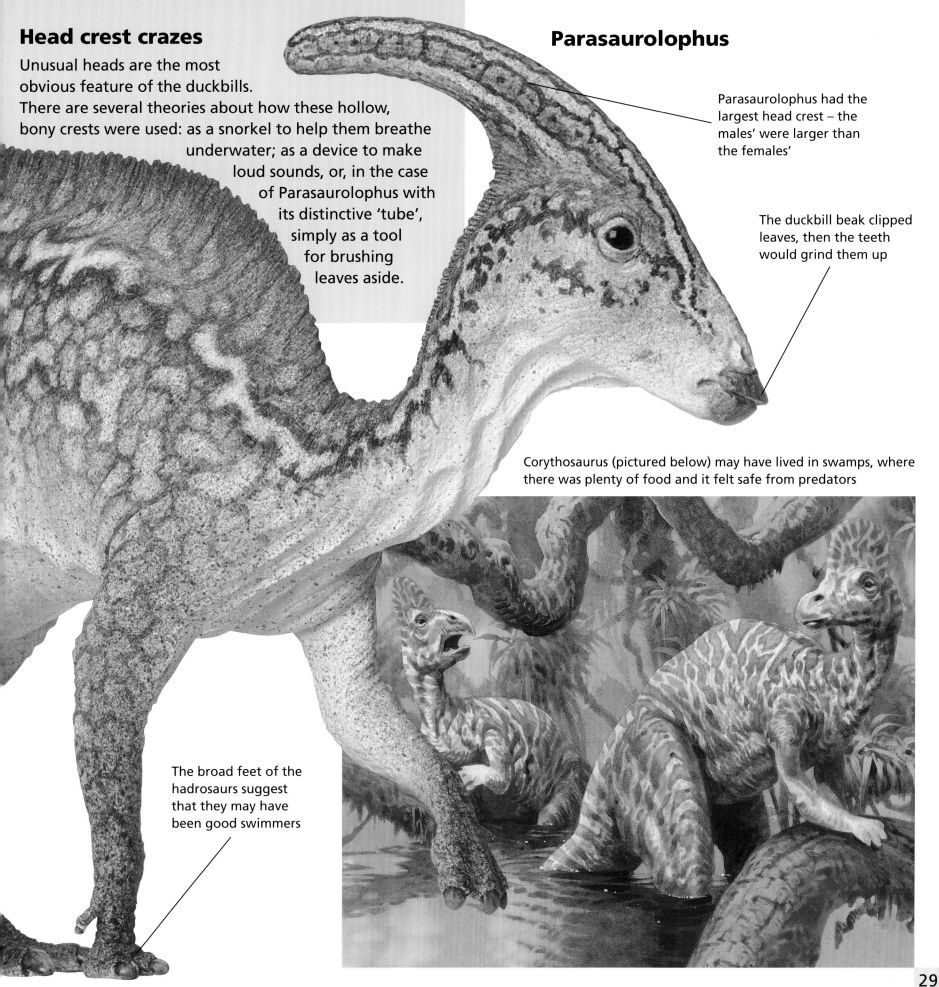

# Head crest crazes

Unusual heads are the most obvious feature of the duckbills. There are several theories about how these hollow, bony crests were used: as a snorkel to help them breathe underwater; as a device to make loud sounds, or, in the case of Parasaurolophus with its distinctive 'tube', simply as a tool for brushing leaves aside.

# Parasaurolophus

Parasaurolophus had the largest head crest – the males' were larger than the females'

The duckbill beak clipped leaves, then the teeth would grind them up

Corythosaurus (pictured below) may have lived in swamps, where there was plenty of food and it felt safe from predators

The broad feet of the hadrosaurs suggest that they may have been good swimmers

# Horns

In the late Cretaceous period, North America was home to a group of beaked, plant-eating dinosaurs known as the ceratopsians. With their large heads, bony neck frills and horns, they are some of the most famous and recognizable dinosaurs that ever lived.

The ceratopsian dinosaurs varied from the size of a dog to the massive, 30-foot long Triceratops. Their most distinctive features were their horns and neck frills (ceratops means 'horned face'). These types of dinosaurs are among those that scientists believe are most likely to have lived in herds. This could have given them increased protection from predators.

**Where?**
Mostly in North America, but some have been found in Mongolia and China

**Diet**
These dinosaurs could have used their sharp beaks to clip off the best parts of plants

**Habitat**
Woodland and open prairie land where they fed on ferns and other fiber-rich plants

**Famous fact**
The five-horned Pentaceratops had the largest skull of any land animal

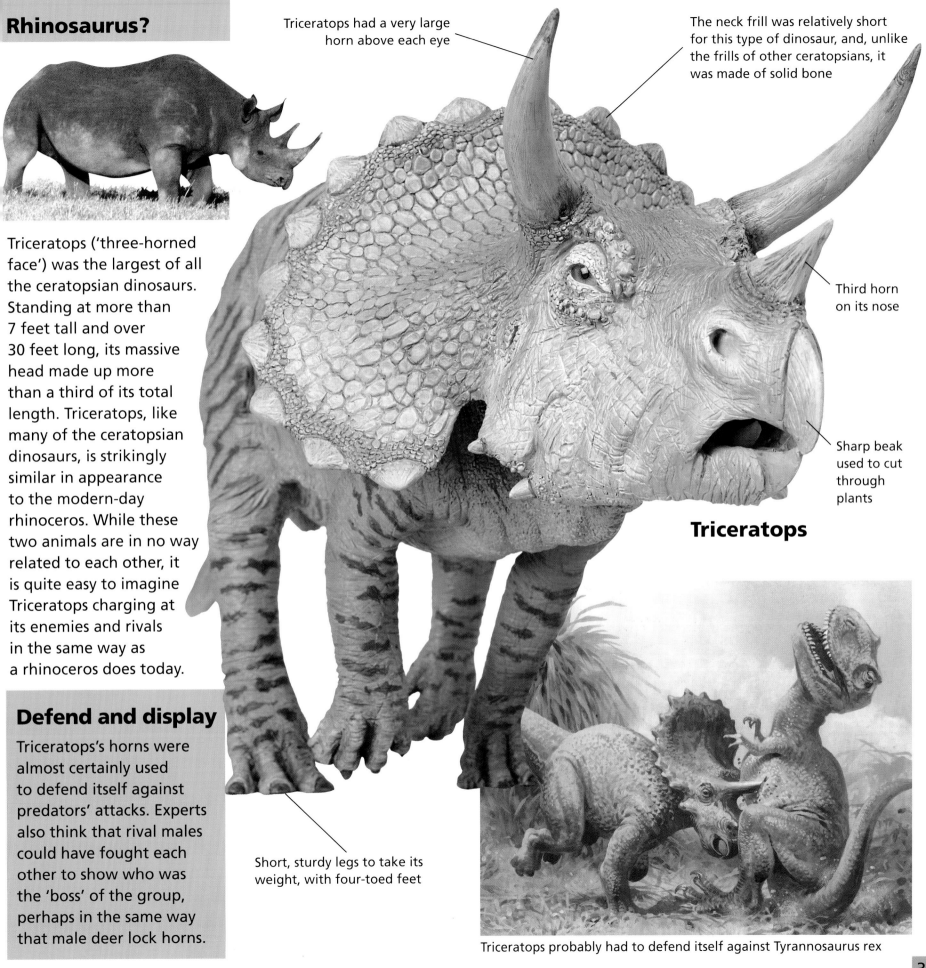

## Rhinosaurus?

Triceratops ('three-horned face') was the largest of all the ceratopsian dinosaurs. Standing at more than 7 feet tall and over 30 feet long, its massive head made up more than a third of its total length. Triceratops, like many of the ceratopsian dinosaurs, is strikingly similar in appearance to the modern-day rhinoceros. While these two animals are in no way related to each other, it is quite easy to imagine Triceratops charging at its enemies and rivals in the same way as a rhinoceros does today.

## Defend and display

Triceratops's horns were almost certainly used to defend itself against predators' attacks. Experts also think that rival males could have fought each other to show who was the 'boss' of the group, perhaps in the same way that male deer lock horns.

Triceratops had a very large horn above each eye

The neck frill was relatively short for this type of dinosaur, and, unlike the frills of other ceratopsians, it was made of solid bone

Third horn on its nose

Sharp beak used to cut through plants

## Triceratops

Short, sturdy legs to take its weight, with four-toed feet

Triceratops probably had to defend itself against Tyrannosaurus rex

## Hollow frills

Chasmosaurus was one of a number of Triceratops's relatives whose frill was even larger than that of Triceratops. There were a number of short, bony spikes around the outside of the frill, which was mostly hollow with skin stretched over it. Its name means 'opening lizard'.

## Common cousin

Chasmosaurus was the most common of the ceratopsians – more examples of it have been found than of any other ceratopsian. Different discoveries have shown big variations in its horns: some have been as long as Triceratops's, others quite short, some have pointed forward, others backward. These could be the differences between males and females.

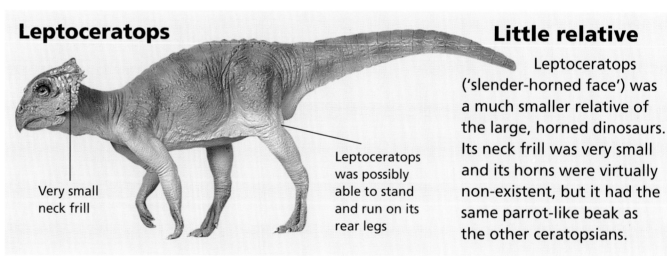

**Chasmosaurus**

## Chasmosaurus

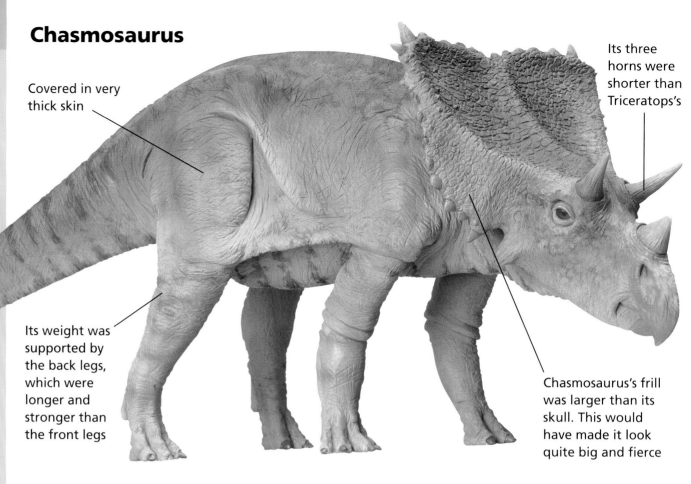

Covered in very thick skin

Its three horns were shorter than Triceratops's

Its weight was supported by the back legs, which were longer and stronger than the front legs

Chasmosaurus's frill was larger than its skull. This would have made it look quite big and fierce

## Leptoceratops

Very small neck frill

Leptoceratops was possibly able to stand and run on its rear legs

## Little relative

Leptoceratops ('slender-horned face') was a much smaller relative of the large, horned dinosaurs. Its neck frill was very small and its horns were virtually non-existent, but it had the same parrot-like beak as the other ceratopsians.

## Horned dinosaurs compared

Chasmosaurus
16 feet long,
7 feet high

Leptoceratops
6.6 feet long,
2.5 feet high

Triceratops
30 feet long,
7 feet high

## Parrot beaks

The ceratopsians are thought to have been some of the most efficient plant-eating dinosaurs. Their very sharp-edged, parrot-like beaks could easily cut into very thick vegetation. They also had sharp, shearing teeth inside their mouths to help them chew through the toughest of meals.

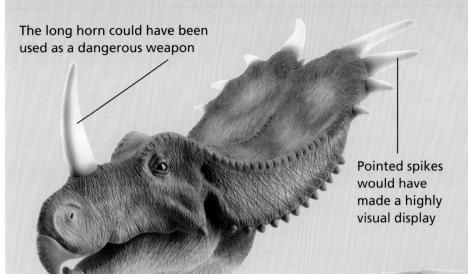

The long horn could have been used as a dangerous weapon

Pointed spikes would have made a highly visual display

## Spiked lizard

Styracosaurus had one of the most spectacular neck frills of all the horned dinosaurs. It had the usual bony nodules at the sides, but there were very long, pointed spikes at the rear of the frill too. Styracosaurus had a single, long horn above its nose.

## Frill uses

The different shapes and sizes of the ceratopsians' horns and neck frills could mean that their main purpose was for identification or display. If these dinosaurs lived in herds then it would have been important for them to recognize each other. Large, hollow frills would have been little use as defense. Some scientists think that the frills simply helped balance their jaws.

## Big frill

Torosaurus had the largest neck frill of any of the ceratopsians, and one of the largest skulls of any land animal that ever lived – Torosaurus skulls have been found measuring up to 8.5 feet in length. Its name means 'perforated lizard', for the holes in its frill.

## Skull spaces

This Chasmosaurus skull shows the large hollows in its neck frill. Many ceratopsian skulls have been found with broken horns, as shown here. This could have been due to fighting.

# Plates and spikes

The stegosaurs were a group of plant eaters that lived in the Jurassic period. They varied in size but all had two rows of plates or spikes (or a combination of the two) running from the back of their necks to their tails.

The rows of tall, bony plates that ran along the stegosaurs' backs gave them their name – 'roof lizards'. Their bodies were large and bulky, and they carried their small heads low and close to the ground. Types included Stegosaurus from North America, the African Kentrosaurus and Tuojiangosaurus from China. They had all died out by the Cretaceous period.

**Where?**
North America, Southern Africa, China and Europe

**Diet**
Leaves and plants that grew close to the ground

**Habitat**
Dense forest areas where there was plenty of food

**Famous fact**
Stegosaurus was once thought to have had a second brain

## Plate lizards

The purpose of the stegosaurs' plates has been debated by scientists. They could have been there to provide protection against attack, or to help the dinosaurs recognize each other (each plate was different). One popular idea is that they helped control body temperature – allowing the dinosaurs to warm up in the sunshine, or to cool down by turning them towards a gentle breeze.

Stegosaurus may have used its rows of back plates as a means of controlling its body temperature

## Spiked defense

Kentrosaurus was a small stegosaur from what is now Africa. Its name means 'sharp point lizard', from the rows of sharp spikes along its back, tail and sides. These could have provided Kentrosaurus with quite an effective means of defending itself. This dinosaur may have reared up on its longer back legs to reach higher plants.

## Plated dinosaurs compared

Stegosaurus
28 feet long,
9 feet high

Tuojiangosaurus
23 feet long,
6 feet high

Kentrosaurus
17 feet long,
6 feet high

Each spike measured up to 2 feet long

## Tuojiangosaurus

This Chinese stegosaur was similar in size to Stegosaurus. It had as many as 30 bony plates arranged in pairs along its neck, back and tail. Like all stegosaurs, it had two pairs of spikes on its tail.

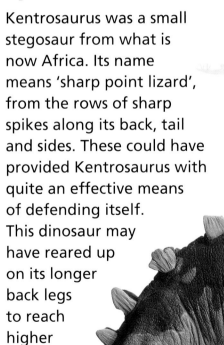
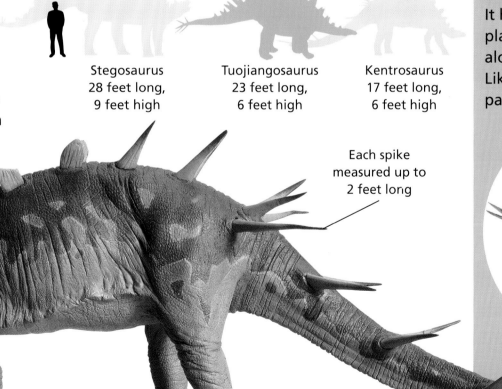

**Kentrosaurus**

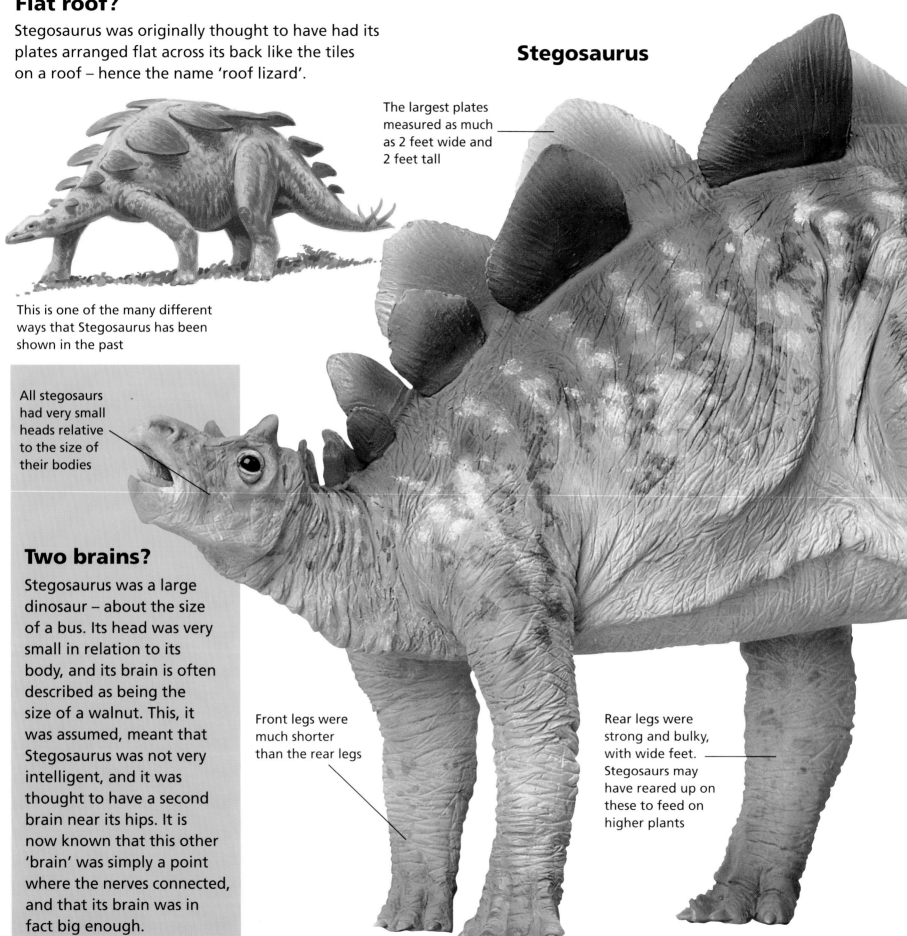

## Flat roof?

Stegosaurus was originally thought to have had its plates arranged flat across its back like the tiles on a roof – hence the name 'roof lizard'.

This is one of the many different ways that Stegosaurus has been shown in the past

**Stegosaurus**

The largest plates measured as much as 2 feet wide and 2 feet tall

All stegosaurs had very small heads relative to the size of their bodies

## Two brains?

Stegosaurus was a large dinosaur – about the size of a bus. Its head was very small in relation to its body, and its brain is often described as being the size of a walnut. This, it was assumed, meant that Stegosaurus was not very intelligent, and it was thought to have a second brain near its hips. It is now known that this other 'brain' was simply a point where the nerves connected, and that its brain was in fact big enough.

Front legs were much shorter than the rear legs

Rear legs were strong and bulky, with wide feet. Stegosaurs may have reared up on these to feed on higher plants

As a means of defense, the plates were too thin to be of much use. They may have been used for display, or to help different groups recognize each other

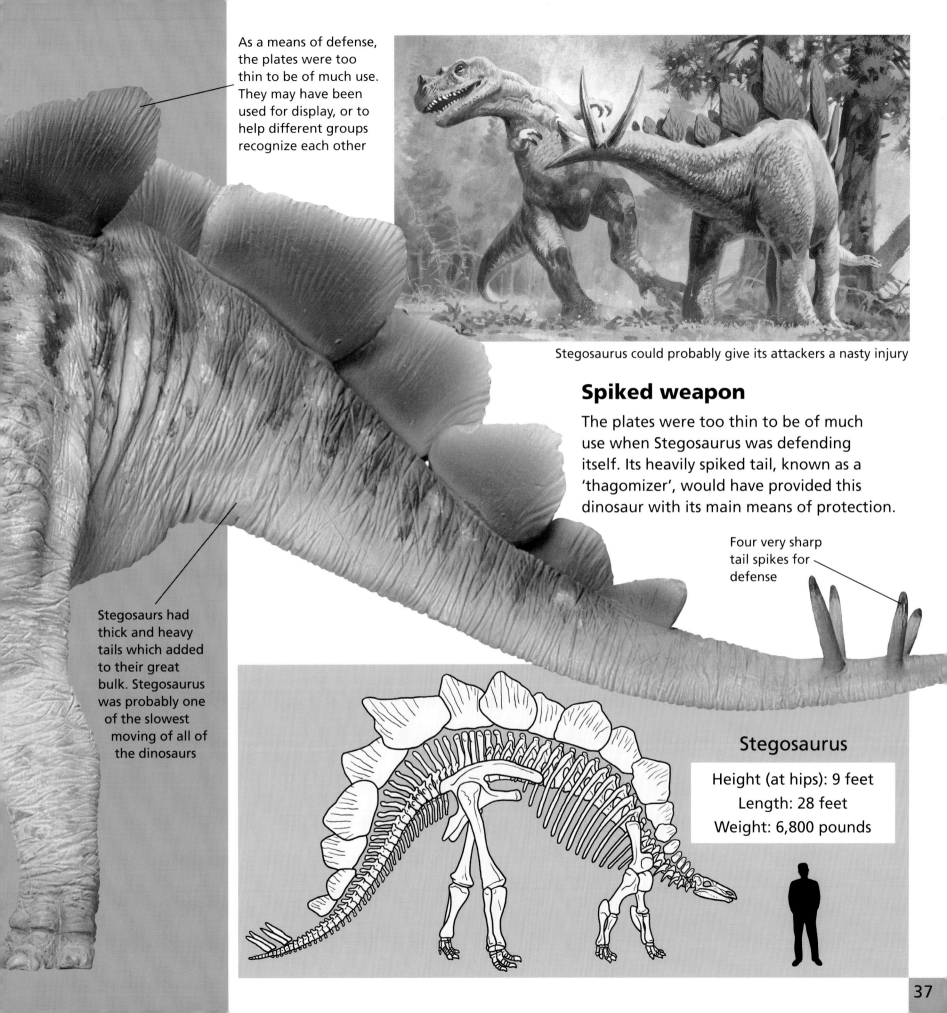

Stegosaurus could probably give its attackers a nasty injury

## Spiked weapon

The plates were too thin to be of much use when Stegosaurus was defending itself. Its heavily spiked tail, known as a 'thagomizer', would have provided this dinosaur with its main means of protection.

Four very sharp tail spikes for defense

Stegosaurs had thick and heavy tails which added to their great bulk. Stegosaurus was probably one of the slowest moving of all of the dinosaurs

### Stegosaurus

Height (at hips): 9 feet
Length: 28 feet
Weight: 6,800 pounds

# Small meat eaters

Smaller meat-eating dinosaurs were in many ways as terrifying, if not more so, than their larger relatives. They ranged from chicken-sized insect eaters to ferocious, man-sized predators that hunted in packs.

A group of small theropods called dromaeosaurs ('running lizards') were some of the fiercest dinosaurs that ever lived. Their teeth were big, curved and razor sharp, and they had vicious claws on their hands and feet that they would use to kill their prey. It is thought that these brutal killers would have been especially effective at hunting in packs.

**Where?**
North America, northern Europe and parts of eastern Asia

**Diet**
The biggest ate larger dinosaurs; others ate small lizards and insects

**Habitat**
They would hunt in open woodland

**Famous fact**
Velociraptor was made famous by the movie *Jurassic Park*

## Terrible claws

The largest dromaeosaur, Deinonychus, was about the same size as a man. Its name means 'terrible claw', after the extra-long claw that all dromaeosaurs had on their second toes. Deinonychus was an impressive predator. Swift on its feet and able to leap powerfully with its rear legs, muscular arms, and long, grasping fingers meant Deinonychus and its relatives could attack almost anything.

Deinonychus would fight viciously with a rival over a kill

## Lethal weapon

The long, sharp claw that the dromaeosaurs had on each second toe claw is one of the most extraordinary features of any dinosaur. This razor-sharp weapon was thought to have been used to slash and cut into its victim with lethal efficiency. Dromaeosaurs could move their second toes separately from the others. They could also hold these toes up to keep them clear of the ground while they were running.

The toe faced down when used to attack unfortunate prey

### Velociraptor

Stripes may have camouflaged this dinosaur in the same way that a tiger is camouflaged today

Long, sharp claws that were curved in shape

## Speedy thief

Velociraptor ('quick robber') was about half the size of its relative Deinonychus. It had a longer, slimmer head than Deinonychus but was equipped with the same lethal range of extremely vicious claws and teeth. Velociraptor lived in what is now Mongolia in Asia, where it probably hunted the smaller ceratopsian dinosaurs.

The toe could be raised up while the other toes remained still

## Small meat eaters compared

Velociraptor
6 feet long,
3 feet high

Troodon
9 feet long,
3 feet high

Archaeopteryx
1.6 feet long,
1 foot high

Dromaeosaurus
6 feet long,
2 feet high

# Dino design

The skeleton of Dromaeosaurus shows some similarities with the large theropods such as Tyrannosaurus rex and Allosaurus

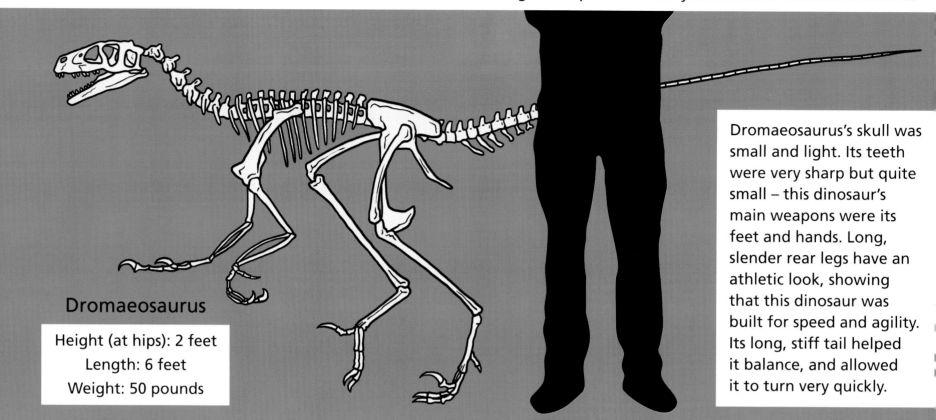

**Dromaeosaurus**

Height (at hips): 2 feet
Length: 6 feet
Weight: 50 pounds

Dromaeosaurus's skull was small and light. Its teeth were very sharp but quite small – this dinosaur's main weapons were its feet and hands. Long, slender rear legs have an athletic look, showing that this dinosaur was built for speed and agility. Its long, stiff tail helped it balance, and allowed it to turn very quickly.

## Running robbers

Before the discovery of Deinonychus and the other small meat eaters, dinosaurs were generally thought to be slow-moving creatures. Now we know that many of these types of raptor ('robber') dinosaur were fast-running. Paleontologists can find out how quickly they could run by studying fossilized trackways of footprints – the distance between each footprint can give an idea of whether the dinosaur was walking or running. Scientists have estimated that these small theropod dinosaurs could possibly have run at speeds of up to 30 mph.

# Wounding tooth

Troodon's curved, saw-edged teeth gave this dinosaur its name – 'wounding tooth'. It had long legs and the same athletic, bird-like features as the dromaeosaurs. It also had a sharp, sickle-like claw on its second toe, but this was not as large as that of Velociraptor and Deinonychus. It probably hunted baby dinosaurs, small reptiles and mammals.

# Bright eyes

Troodon's eyes faced forward which meant that its vision was highly developed. This helped it to focus and judge distances – very important when hunting small, fast-moving prey.

**Troodon**

Large pupils may have allowed Troodon to hunt at night

# Intelligence

Troodon had the largest brain of any dinosaur, relative to its size. This suggests that it was the most intelligent of all the dinosaurs. Most of its extra brain power was given to handling its probably advanced senses of smell and taste, and greater control of its limbs and reflexes. All of this enabled it to become a very effective hunter. It's possible that Troodon would have planned its attacks, perhaps hiding until the time was right to catch its prey.

# Dinosaur bird

Archaeopteryx was an unusual creature from the late Jurassic period, and could show a link between dinosaurs and birds. About the size of a large crow, it had wings and feathers like a bird and could possibly fly. It had arms, claws and teeth that were very similar to those of the small theropod dinosaurs.

Feathered wings

Long claws with three fingers

# Small and speedy

Just as there were small, fast, meat-eating predators, other small, fast-moving dinosaurs appeared during the late Jurassic period. Some of these dinosaurs ate only plants; other bird-like types were omnivorous (also eating insects and small animals).

Like the other small dinosaurs, this group of speedy creatures were bipedal, walking and running on two legs. The group shown here are Hypsilophodon. About the same size as Velociraptor, their bodies were built for running quickly, and they probably traveled in small herds, feeding on low-lying vegetation as they found it – somewhat similar to the way modern deer do today.

**Where?**
Hypsilophodon was first found in England and later found in South Dakota, USA

**Diet**
Plants close to the ground. Some types may also have eaten insects

**Habitat**
Hypsilophodon liked woodland; the 'ostrich dinosaurs' lived in a desert-like region

**Famous fact**
The 'ostrich dinosaurs' were probably the speediest dinosaurs

Though quick, these dinosaurs were still at risk from large predators

## Bird mimics

The ornithomimids ('bird mimics') were very similar in many ways to ostriches, and are often known as the 'ostrich dinosaurs'. They had very long, slender legs and bird-like, toothless beaks. One of the biggest of the 'ostrich dinosaurs' was Gallimimus, which lived in Asia during the late Cretaceous period.

Gallimimus

## Running pose

Ornithomimus was smaller than Gallimimus, but shared its forward-pointing pose and stiffened tail as it ran. Large, forward-facing eyes probably gave it very good vision.

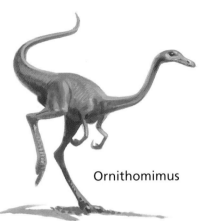
Ornithomimus

## Zephyrosaurus

It stood and ran on two legs

Mouth and teeth were highly adapted to chewing quickly

Long, stiff tail to help it balance

## Windy lizard

Zephyrosaurus ('west-wind lizard') was a relative of Hypsilophodon from early Cretaceous North America.

## Dino sprinters

The ostrich is one of the fastest living animals, running at up to 50 mph. Many scientists think that Gallimimus and its relatives could run as fast as that, and that their long, sprinter's legs may even have been able to take them faster in short bursts of speed.

### Fast runners compared

Gallimimus
20 feet long,
10 feet high

Zephyrosaurus
6 feet long,
3 feet high

Ornithomimus
17 feet long,
7 feet high

43

# Armor and defense

When the plated stegosaurs died out at the end of the Jurassic period, they were replaced by the ankylosaurs. These very slow-moving, low-level, tank-like plant eaters relied on various combinations of bony armor, spikes and clubbed tails to protect themselves.

The most heavily armored of the ankylosaurs included Euoplocephalus ('well-armored head'). This dinosaur was very common in late Cretaceous North America, where it would graze on plants as it moved slowly along. Its most distinctive feature was the massive, bony tail club which it would use to swing at its predators.

**Where?**
North America, with some relatives discovered in Australia

**Diet**
Plants that grew close to the ground

**Habitat**
Mostly in open woodland areas

**Famous fact**
Some ankylosaurs even had bony eyelids

# Armored tank

Euoplocephalus was protected by very thick skin, which in turn was covered by bands of thick, flexible bony plates. Rows of bony studs ran along its back and sides, with the occasional spike for good measure. Its skull was extremely thick and heavy, with a pattern of bony plates that looked like paving slabs across the top. It even had bony eyelids that flicked up and down to protect its eyes. Such protection gave Euoplocephalus its name, which means 'well-armored head'.

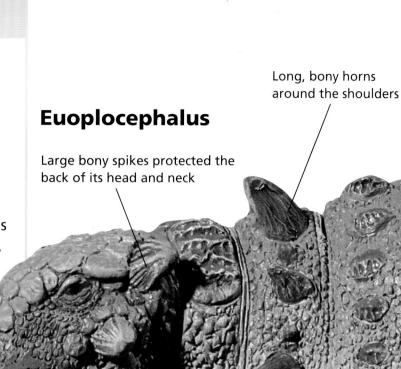

## Euoplocephalus

Large bony spikes protected the back of its head and neck

Long, bony horns around the shoulders

Armored plates were arranged in rows of flexible bands

Wide, toothless beak for clipping vegetation

Wide, muscular legs to support its massive weight

### Euoplocephalus

Height (at hips): 6 feet
Length: 20 feet
Weight: 4,000 pounds

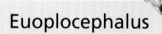

# Armored dinosaurs compared

| Nodosaurus | Sauropelta | Euoplocephalus | Ankylosaurus | Scelidosaurus |
|---|---|---|---|---|
| 16 feet long, 5 feet high | 25 feet long, 6 feet high | 20 feet long, 6 feet high | 30 feet long, 5 feet high | 13 feet long, 4 feet high |

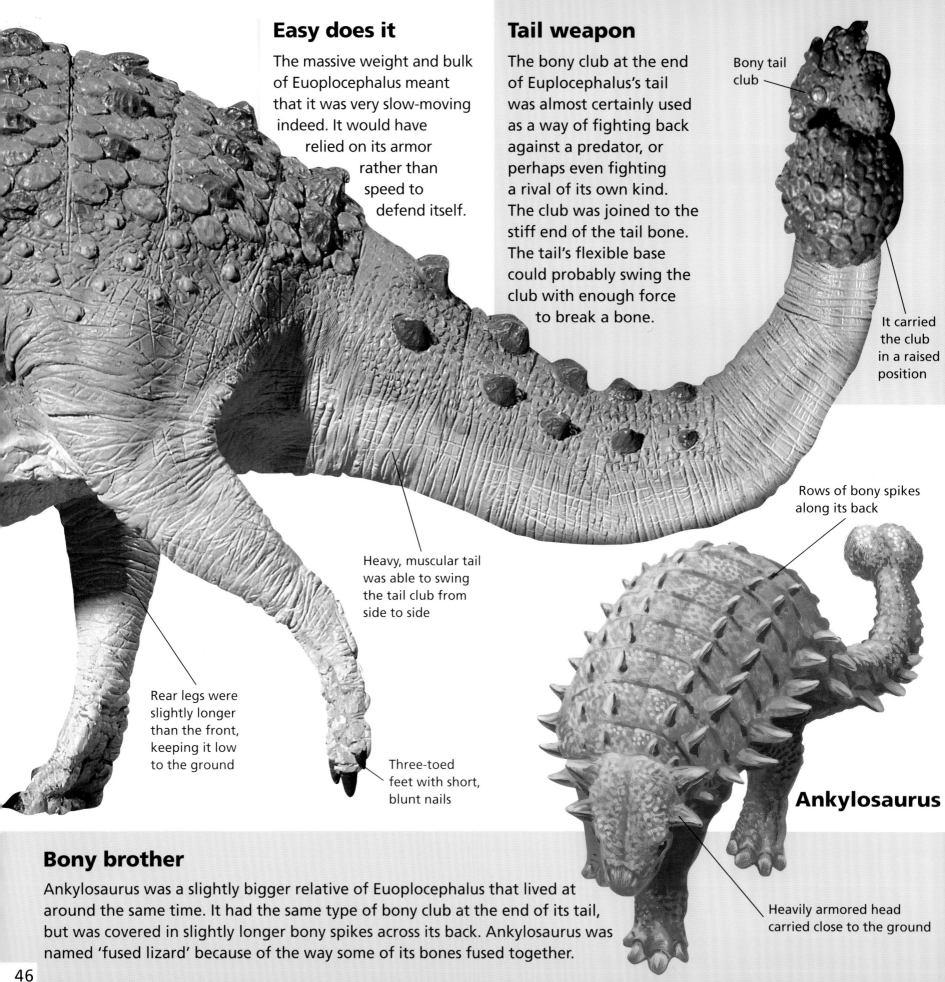

## Easy does it

The massive weight and bulk of Euoplocephalus meant that it was very slow-moving indeed. It would have relied on its armor rather than speed to defend itself.

## Tail weapon

The bony club at the end of Euplocephalus's tail was almost certainly used as a way of fighting back against a predator, or perhaps even fighting a rival of its own kind. The club was joined to the stiff end of the tail bone. The tail's flexible base could probably swing the club with enough force to break a bone.

Bony tail club

It carried the club in a raised position

Rows of bony spikes along its back

Heavy, muscular tail was able to swing the tail club from side to side

Rear legs were slightly longer than the front, keeping it low to the ground

Three-toed feet with short, blunt nails

**Ankylosaurus**

Heavily armored head carried close to the ground

## Bony brother

Ankylosaurus was a slightly bigger relative of Euoplocephalus that lived at around the same time. It had the same type of bony club at the end of its tail, but was covered in slightly longer bony spikes across its back. Ankylosaurus was named 'fused lizard' because of the way some of its bones fused together.

Euoplocephalus could have used its weapons to fight each other

## Early relative

Scelidosaurus was an early relative of the heavily armored ankylosaurs that lived in the early Jurassic period in England. It was much smaller and lighter than the tank-like Euoplocephalus, with small bony 'scutes' across its back.

Bony armor across back and tail

Small head was not well protected

Nodosaurus

## First find

Nodosaurus was one of the first of the ankylosaurs to be discovered. It was one of the least armored dinosaurs of its kind, with only its back covered in tightly-packed bony plates. It may have dropped low to the ground to protect itself when it was attacked.

Sauropelta

## Node lizards

Sauropelta was an early example of a nodosaur – slightly less armored types of ankylosaurs. It had no tail club, but rows of bony 'scutes' protected its back. Two rows of bony spikes ran back from its shoulders.

Scelidosaurus – a very early ankylosaur

47

# Bone heads

The pachycephalosaurs ('thick-headed reptiles') were a group of dinosaurs with extra-thick bones on the tops of their skulls. The best known types, such as Pachycephalosaurus, had a rounded, dome-shaped skull. Others, like Homalocephale, had a more flattened shape.

It was once thought that rival male 'bone heads' would use their heads to butt each other head first in a way similar to goats and sheep. Most scientists now think this would have caused too much damage to the dinosaurs' necks, and consider it more likely that the pachycephalosaurs used their heads to push into the sides of others.

**Where?**
Pachycephalosaurus and Stegoceras are from North America

**Diet**
Leaves, fruits, berries, and perhaps some small animals

**Habitat**
These dinosaurs lived in heavily forested areas

**Famous fact**
Micropachycephalosaurus, from China, has the longest dinosaur name

# Bone head giant

Most pachycephalosaurs were small – smaller than the average human being. Pachycephalosaurus was the big exception – it walked on its rear legs and stood up to 15 feet tall. It would stand upright to feed from trees, or crouch down low to graze on plants close to the ground. It had quite slim legs and feet and was probably able to run at a good speed. The skeleton below shows Pachycephalosaurus in running pose, perhaps ready to charge at a rival.

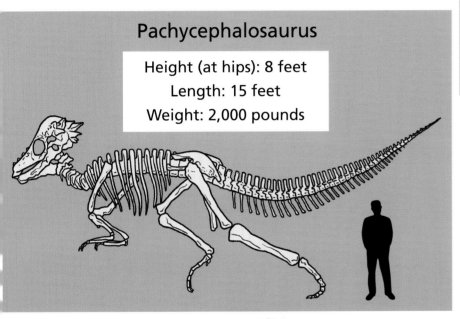

## Pachycephalosaurus

Height (at hips): 8 feet
Length: 15 feet
Weight: 2,000 pounds

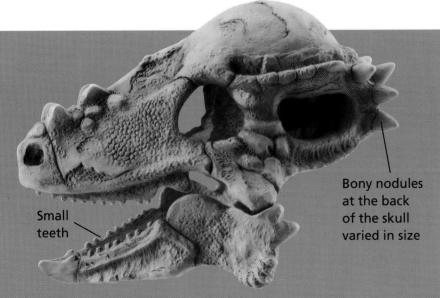

Small teeth

Bony nodules at the back of the skull varied in size

# Knobbly dome

Pachycephalosaur skulls vary in shape from animal to animal. This Pachycephalosaurus skull had bony nodules above the nose and at the back of the skull.

# Flat head

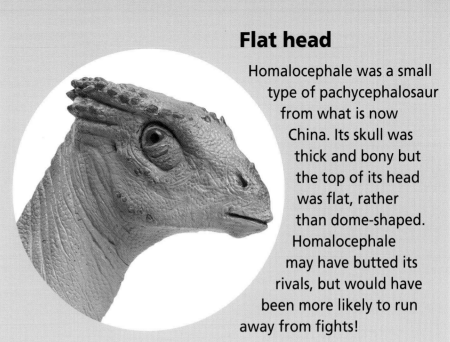

Homalocephale was a small type of pachycephalosaur from what is now China. Its skull was thick and bony but the top of its head was flat, rather than dome-shaped. Homalocephale may have butted its rivals, but would have been more likely to run away from fights!

# Horned roof

Stegoceras ('horned roof') was the first of the pachycephalosaurs to be discovered. This picture shows the domed head that these dinosaurs are famous for.

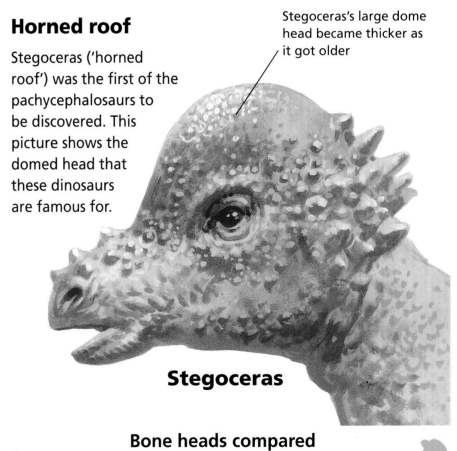

Stegoceras's large dome head became thicker as it got older

## Stegoceras

## Bone heads compared

Stegoceras
8 feet long,
4 feet high

Homalocephale
5 feet long,
2 feet high

Pachycephalosaurus
15 feet long,
8 feet high

# Sea reptiles

At the same time that the dinosaurs lived on land, many kinds of strange reptiles lived in the seas. These creatures varied in size and shape, but the two best-known groups were the plesiosaurs and ichthyosaurs. Both lived from the Triassic to the Cretaceous periods.

Plesiosaurs can be divided up into two groups – pliosaurs and elasmosaurs. Pliosaurs were short-necked, broad and muscular-looking with very large heads. Elasmosaurs had much longer necks and bodies. Ichthyosaurs were smaller, and closely resembled modern-day fish and dolphins.

**Where?**
North America, Europe, Australia and South America

**Diet**
Fish and shellfish. Pliosaurs also ate other sea reptiles

**Habitat**
These sea reptiles swam and hunted in deep oceans

**Famous fact**
Some people claim to have seen plesiosaur-like creatures in modern times

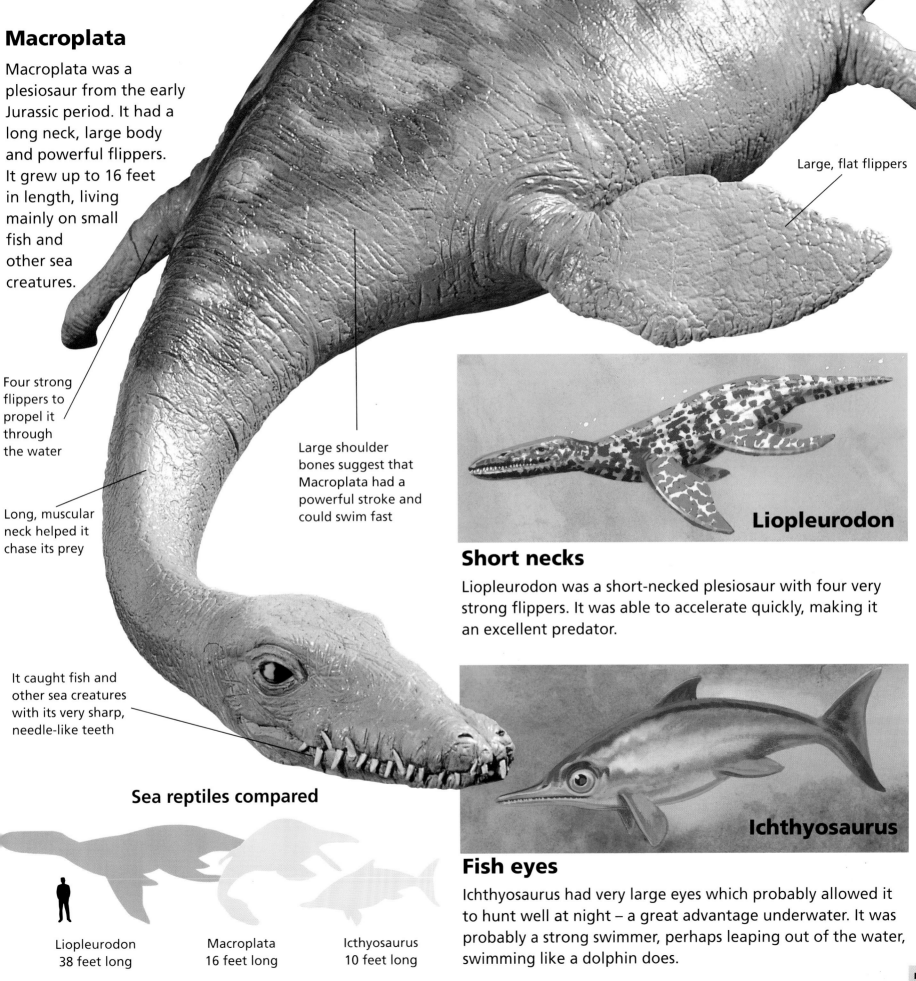

# Macroplata

Macroplata was a plesiosaur from the early Jurassic period. It had a long neck, large body and powerful flippers. It grew up to 16 feet in length, living mainly on small fish and other sea creatures.

Four strong flippers to propel it through the water

Long, muscular neck helped it chase its prey

It caught fish and other sea creatures with its very sharp, needle-like teeth

Large shoulder bones suggest that Macroplata had a powerful stroke and could swim fast

Large, flat flippers

**Liopleurodon**

## Short necks

Liopleurodon was a short-necked plesiosaur with four very strong flippers. It was able to accelerate quickly, making it an excellent predator.

**Ichthyosaurus**

## Fish eyes

Ichthyosaurus had very large eyes which probably allowed it to hunt well at night – a great advantage underwater. It was probably a strong swimmer, perhaps leaping out of the water, swimming like a dolphin does.

## Sea reptiles compared

Liopleurodon
38 feet long

Macroplata
16 feet long

Icthyosaurus
10 feet long

# Flying reptiles

Pterosaurs were flying reptiles which may have been related to the dinosaurs that lived at the same time. They appeared in the Triassic period and died out with the dinosaurs. Some of the later pterosaurs were the largest flying creatures that have ever lived.

 Pterosaurs had wings made of leathery skin, which stretched from the end of a very long fourth finger to their bodies and back legs. Early types were relatively small, with large heads and toothed beaks. The later, more advanced pterosaurs (the pterodactyloids) were larger, with long, narrow heads. Many of them had large, toothless beaks.

**Where?**
Most pterosaurs have been found in Europe and North America

**Diet**
Insects, fish and small animals. They may have scavenged from large dead animals

**Habitat**
Beaches and the shorelines of woodland rivers

**Famous fact**
'Pterodactyl' is an often-used but incorrect name for pterosaurs

# Kings of the sky

Many pterosaur fossils have been discovered and studied. Scientists have found that even the most primitive types were quite sophisticated for creatures of that time. The ability to fly requires both good vision and an excellent sense of balance. Pterosaurs had large eyes and well-developed brains, similar to those of modern birds.

## Dimorphodon

Dimorphodon was an early Jurassic pterosaur with an especially large skull and a long, stiffened tail. It probably preyed on small reptiles and fish whenever it had a chance.

## Rhamphorynchus

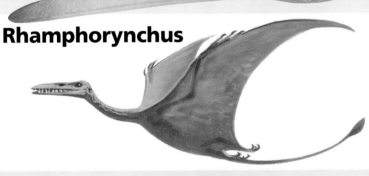

Rhamphorynchus had a long, slim beak with several long teeth that pointed forward. These probably helped it to scoop up fish as it swooped low over the water.

## Pteranodon

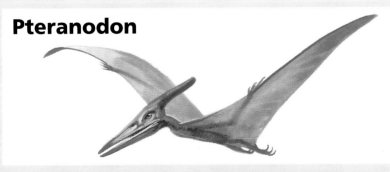

Pteranodon is one of the best-known pterosaurs. It was large, with a big crest at the back of its head. It probably had a pouch under its bill, rather like that of a pelican.

Like all pterosaurs, Pteranodon was a capable predator, swooping down to catch fish

## Quetzalcoatlus

Longest neck of all pterosaurs

Three clawed fingers for grabbing hold of prey

### Giant glider

Quetzalcoatlus was the biggest pterosaur. The size of a small aircraft, it was the largest flying creature that has ever lived.

## Pterosaurs compared

| Pteranodon wingspan: 30 feet | Dimorphodon wingspan: 3.5 feet | Quetzalcoatlus wingspan: 40 feet | Rhamphorynchus wingspan: 15 feet |

# Dinosaur extinction

The last of the dinosaurs died out around 65 million years ago in a mass extinction that wiped out 50 percent of all the living things on Earth. There are a number of theories about what caused this to happen, and scientists continue to debate these ideas.

Both the Triassic and Jurassic periods ended with some dinosaurs and other living things becoming extinct, but it was the end of the Cretaceous period that saw the mass extinction of the dinosaurs. Species become extinct when they cannot adapt to changes, compete with other species, or when something catastrophic happens. This is a part of the process of evolution.

**Where?**
The mass extinction affected the entire planet

**Diet**
Any event that limited food supply would have had a dramatic impact

**Habitat**
A number of things could have caused environmental changes

**Famous fact**
Species continue to become extinct, even today

## Impact theory

The best-known theory of how the dinosaurs were wiped out is that a huge asteroid crashed into the Earth. This impact would have had a devastating effect on the planet, and the explosions would have killed millions of living things instantly. Vast amounts of dust thrown into the atmosphere would have blocked out the sun's light, causing plants to die out and the temperature to drop. As a result, food would have become scarce, and dinosaurs and other animals unable to adapt would have died out.

An impact crater in Arizona, USA

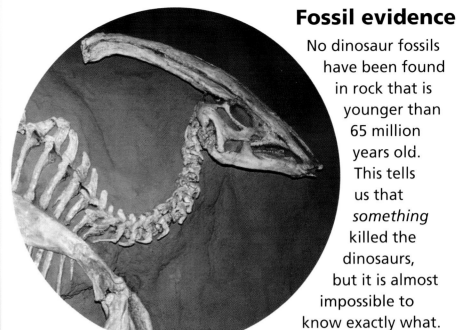

## Fossil evidence

No dinosaur fossils have been found in rock that is younger than 65 million years old. This tells us that *something* killed the dinosaurs, but it is almost impossible to know exactly what.

Major volcanic activity may have been caused by an asteroid impact

## Gradual changes

The massive and sudden devastation caused by an asteroid impact may not be the only explanation for the end of the dinosaurs.

The Earth was changing in the millions of years leading up to the end of the Cretaceous period. The continents were shifting, and the climate changed dramatically in a relatively short period of time – about 20,000 years.

It could be that because the dinosaurs were already struggling to adapt to these changes to their habitat and climate, a sudden catastrophe such as the asteroid impact killed off an already struggling species. It was almost certainly not the case that the dinosaurs were alive one day and all dead the next. Evolution happens over many millions of years.

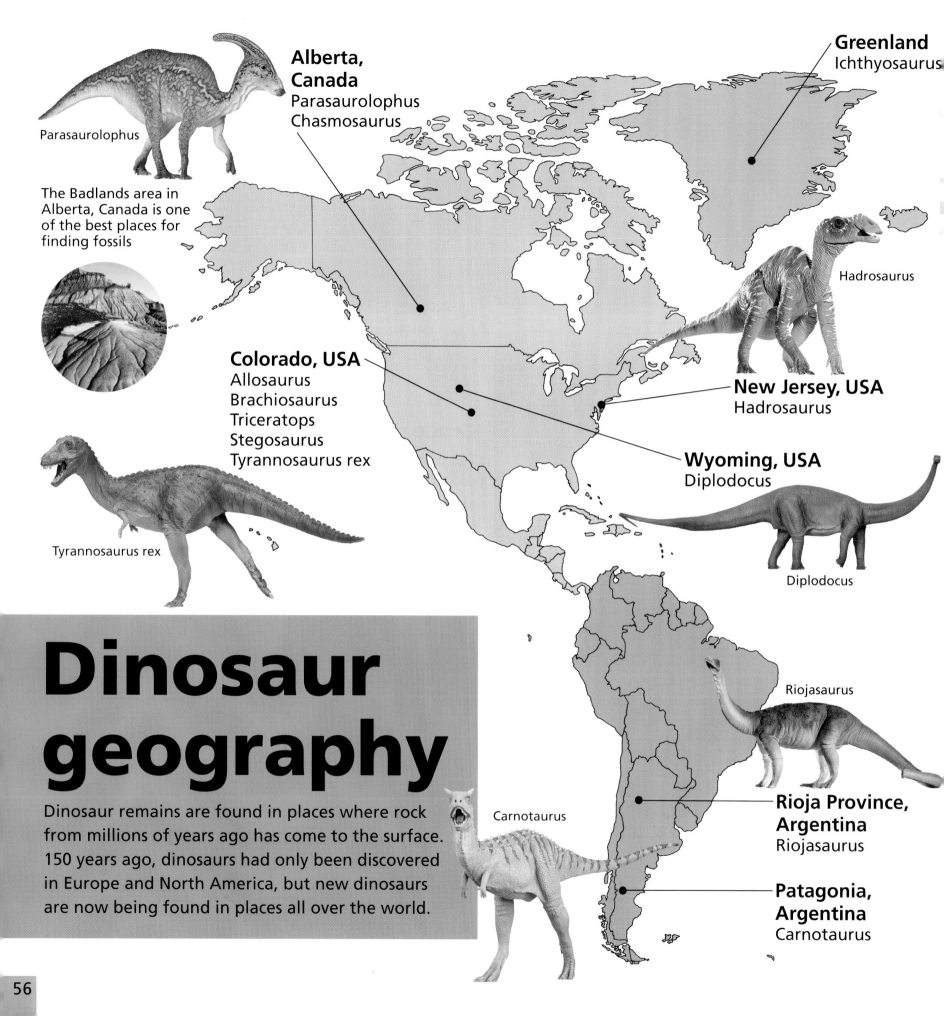

**Alberta, Canada**
Parasaurolophus
Chasmosaurus

Parasaurolophus

The Badlands area in Alberta, Canada is one of the best places for finding fossils

**Greenland**
Ichthyosaurus

Hadrosaurus

**Colorado, USA**
Allosaurus
Brachiosaurus
Triceratops
Stegosaurus
Tyrannosaurus rex

**New Jersey, USA**
Hadrosaurus

**Wyoming, USA**
Diplodocus

Tyrannosaurus rex

Diplodocus

# Dinosaur geography

Dinosaur remains are found in places where rock from millions of years ago has come to the surface. 150 years ago, dinosaurs had only been discovered in Europe and North America, but new dinosaurs are now being found in places all over the world.

Carnotaurus

Riojasaurus

**Rioja Province, Argentina**
Riojasaurus

**Patagonia, Argentina**
Carnotaurus

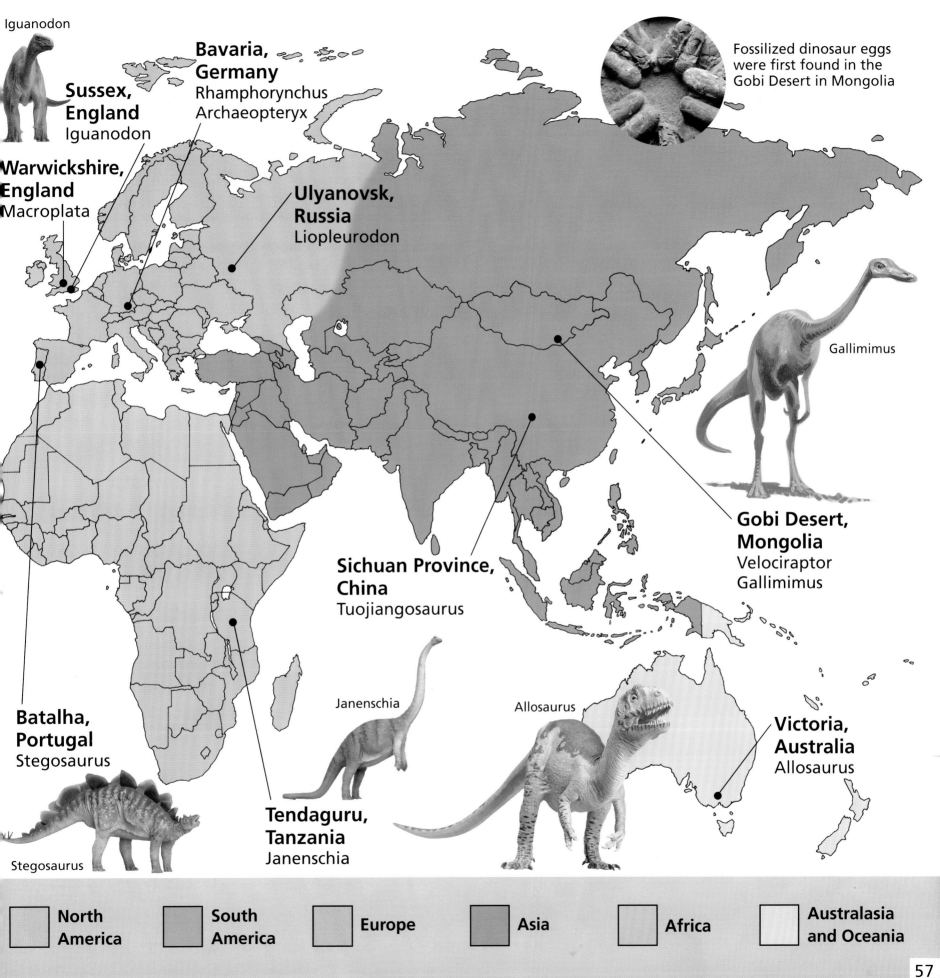

Iguanodon

**Sussex,
England**
Iguanodon

**Bavaria,
Germany**
Rhamphorynchus
Archaeopteryx

**Warwickshire,
England**
Macroplata

**Ulyanovsk,
Russia**
Liopleurodon

Fossilized dinosaur eggs
were first found in the
Gobi Desert in Mongolia

Gallimimus

**Gobi Desert,
Mongolia**
Velociraptor
Gallimimus

**Sichuan Province,
China**
Tuojiangosaurus

Janenschia

Allosaurus

**Victoria,
Australia**
Allosaurus

**Batalha,
Portugal**
Stegosaurus

Stegosaurus

**Tendaguru,
Tanzania**
Janenschia

**North
America**

**South
America**

**Europe**

**Asia**

**Africa**

**Australasia
and Oceania**

# Glossary

## Amphibian

An animal that can live on land or in water, such as a frog. Amphibians are cold-blooded, which means their body temperature changes along with the temperature of their surroundings. The earliest amphibians appeared in the **Jurassic period.**

## Ankylosaur

A group of heavily built, plant-eating dinosaurs that lived in the **Cretaceous period.** They were covered with bony armor, spikes and had clubbed tails. Euplocephalus was a type of ankylosaur.

## Asteroid

A rocky object that orbits the Sun. One popular theory about how the dinosaurs became **extinct** is that an asteroid struck the Earth about 65 million years ago.

## Bipedal

An animal that stands and walks on two legs is bipedal. Dinosaurs such as Allosaurus and Tyrannosaurus rex were bipedal dinosaurs.

## Camouflage

Features or patterns that make plants and animals look like their surroundings. Camouflage is useful because it allows plants and animals to hide from their enemies. Velociraptor was a dinosaur which may have been well camouflaged with stripes a bit like a tiger.

## Cannibal

An animal that eats the flesh of another animal of the same species. Some dinosaurs, such as Allosaurus, were thought to be cannibals.

## Carnivore

An animal that eats meat. Many of the dinosaurs were carnivores, such as Deinonychus and Velociraptor. Animals that do not eat meat are called **herbivores.**

## Ceratopsian

A group of plant-eating dinosaurs which had sharp beaks, large heads, bony neck frills and horns. Triceratops and Chasmosaurus were ceratopsian dinosaurs.

## Cretaceous period

This was the last period of time during which dinosaurs lived on Earth. The Cretaceous period began about 144 million years ago and ended 79 million years later with the **extinction** of the dinosaurs.

## Dromaeosaur

A small, fierce, meat-eating group of **theropods** which lived in the late **Cretaceous period.** They were **bipedal,** and had large, slashing claws on their hind feet which they used to attack prey. Velociraptor was a type of dromaeosaur.

## Evolution

The theory of evolution is that all the varieties of plants and animals that exist today have developed over many millions of years from earlier types, and that their differences arose from changes made over time.

## Extinct

When an entire species (or type of animal) dies out, the species becomes extinct. The dinosaurs became extinct around 65 million years ago.

## Fossil

The remains or impression of a plant or animal that has been preserved for many years in rock. We study dinosaurs from fossils that have been found.

## Gastrolith

A small stone, swallowed by an animal to help it digest food. Many **sauropods** used gastroliths because they found it hard to chew food into small pieces.

## Hadrosaur

A group of large, plant-eating dinosaurs, with duck-like bills. Hadrosaurus was a hadrosaur.

## Herbivore

An animal that feeds on plants, and does not eat the meat of other animals.

## Icthyosaur

A group of marine **reptiles** that lived in the seas at the same time as the dinosaurs.

## Jurassic period

The period of time which lasted from 203 to 144 million years ago. Diplodocus and other well-known dinosaurs appeared during this period.

## Mammal

The name given to all animals of which the female gives birth to live young, and produces her own milk to feed them with. Humans are mammals.

## Omnivore

An animal that eats both plants and the meat of other animals. Many dinosaurs were omivores, such as Gallimimus.

## Paleontology

The scientific study of **fossilized** animals or plants. A person who studies paleontology is called a paleontologist.

## Plesiosaur

A group of marine **reptiles** that lived in the seas at the same time as the dinosaurs. Macroplata was a plesiosaur.

## Predator

An animal that captures, kills, and eats other animals. The animal that is caught by a predator is called the **prey.** Dinosaurs could be both predators, and **prey** for other predators.

## Prey

An animal hunted by another animal for food. The animal that hunts prey is called the **predator.**

## Pterosaur

A group of flying **reptiles** that lived at the same time as dinosaurs. Dimorphodon and Quetzalcoatlus were types of pterosaurs.

## Reptile

The name given to all animals with a dry, scaly skin. Reptiles are cold-blooded, which means their body temperature changes along with the temperature of their surroundings. Many kinds of reptiles, such as the dinosaurs, have died out.

## Sauropod

A group of very large **herbivorous** dinosaurs with long necks and tails, large limbs and a small head. Sauropods were the largest animals that have ever lived. Diplodocus was a sauropod.

## Scute

A thick, horny or bony plate on an animal's back. Sauropelta's body was covered in scutes.

## Stegosaur

A group of plant-eating dinosaurs that lived in the **Jurassic period,** with plates or spikes along their backs. Stegosaurus was a stegosaur.

## Theropod

A large group of meat-eating dinosaurs that were **bipedal** and ranged in size. Dromaeosaurus was a small theropod, Tyrannosaurus rex was a large theropod.

## Triassic period

The period of time that started about 250 million years ago and ended about 42 million years later. The first dinosaurs appeared towards the end of the Triassic period.

## Vegetarian

An animal that does not eat meat or fish, but only plant and vegetable matter. Kentrosaurus was vegetarian.

# Web directory

If you want to discover more fascinating facts about dinosaurs, here is our pick of the best dinosaur sites on the web:

**www.nhm.ac.uk/nature-online/life/dinosaurs-other-extinct-creatures**
Use the Dino Directory to search for dinosaurs by country, time, body shape or in alphabetical order.

**paleobiology.si.edu/dinosaurs/index.html**
Answers to frequently asked dinosaur questions, a look at common misconceptions, and a virtual dinosaur dig.

**www.ucmp.berkeley.edu/diapsids/dinosaur.html**
Experts attempt to separate fact from fiction by looking at how dinosaurs are portrayed in movies.

**www.enchantedlearning.com/subjects/dinosaurs**
Information on virtually every dinosaur with maps, records and fact sheets to print out.

**dsc.discovery.com/guides/dinosaur/dinosaur.html**
Interactive site that lets you explore 20 of the best-known dinosaurs in 3-D.

# Index